Hugo Wormsbecher

# Our Courtyard

*(Short novel)*

Translated from German by Dr. Walther Friesen

2019
Dortmund

Editor: Artem Scheller Medienagentur.
*Reference address: Mastbruch 3, 44357 Dortmund*
*Tel.: +49 231/580 691 18*
*E-Mail: schellerartem@gmail.com*

Printing and publishing: BoD – Books on Demand, Norderstedt.

**ISBN 978-3-75042-980-2**

**Hugo Wormsbecher**

*"Due to the beginning of the war, the dissolution of the Volga-German Autonomous Republic, the expulsion of the Germans from Ukraine, Crimea, the Volga region, the Caucasus, Moscow and Leningrad to Siberia and Kazakhstan, the development of the Soviet-German Literature was disrupted for many years. The wartime, the years of labour service, when the entire adult German population — both men and women — was in camps behind barbed wire, where thousands and thousands died, were not just the years when nothing could be published. Those were the years of deep silence..."*

Hugo Wormsbecher. Having gone through all the hardships with the people/ Mit dem Volk durch alle Härten gegangen (Notes on Soviet German Literature/Notizen über die sowjetdeutsche Literatur); journal ‚Heimatliche Weiten', № 1/1989.

*"The short novel 'Our Courtyard' was written long before the Perestroika period, but its publication had been banned for 15 years. But even after its release in the journal 'Heimatliche Weiten', it remained under supervision for a long time."*

Nina Paulsen, Dr. Walther Friesen. Hugo Wormsbecher's 'Our Courtyard' on stage for the first time / Unser Hof' erstmals auf der Theaterbühne; journal ‚Volk auf dem Weg' Nr. 1/2018.

*„According to reliable information that has been gathered by military authorities, there are thousands and tens of thousands of saboteurs and spies among the German population living in different districts of the Volga Region who at a given signal from Germany must carry out explosions in the areas that are inhabited by the Volga Germans. ...The State Defense Committee ... must urgently carry out the resettlement of all the Volga Germans..."*
(From the Decree of the Presidium of the Supreme Soviet of the USSR of 28 August 1941)

# 1. Father's Footprint

It stopped raining long ago and I'd like to go out. Maybe little Hans is already out there. Maybe little Karl is also there. And Elsa, too. I'm feeling bored at home, but to go out wouldn't be good, 'cause others also want to do it, but they don't go out. We are staying in, 'cause of our father. He's sitting at the table, with his hands on it, and he's looking at them. He's been sitting so for quite a long time. Mother is sitting opposite to him and she's also looking at father's hands. Arno's seated himself by the stove. He's tilted his body sideways to the table, and hanged his head, as if staring at the floor. But I see that he's casting side glances at our father.

Now and then, he takes a look at him and then drops his eyes again. Only his hair on the crown is sticking up. And Maria is lulling her stuffed puppet with purple eyes that she painted with a chemical pencil as we still lived at home.

I can see everything very well, 'cause I've rolled my tiny log to the window, climbed on it, and now I'm looking by turns at the street through the window or at the room.

Every one of us has got his own loglet. Grandpa Semenych who lives next door has sawn out them for us. I like my loglet. It's got very polished. 'Cause I'm always twirling on it and so I'm rubbing off the only pants I've got...

I'm looking out of the window. The sun has risen already at one spot.

"It's sunny now," I say.

"Be quiet, Fritzik," Mother says.

I sigh. Mother never says anything to no purpose. It means I have to keep silent. And stay at home.

My father goes far away today. There's a village there. And Volodya's father is also going there, and little Karl's father, and Elsa's. And fathers of all the boys I know are going to that far away village. Only Otto's father doesn't go there, 'cause his father is at the front. And fathers of all Russian children are also at the front.

Our fathers are leaving for work. There should be plenty of work to be done there, that's why so many of them are going there. Though, there is also a lot of work to be done in our village, 'cause when we get up in the morning our father is never at home. He comes only when Mother closes the window with the shutters, so that nobody could see from the street how we're sitting down to supper.

Maybe, there're indeed very many children in the village my father is going to, 'cause my father is a teacher and he said, "All of us would be needed there..." That means that a teacher would also be needed there, and my father would teach children there.

Elsa's father is also a teacher. But he isn't the kind of teacher like my father. My father is a teacher of Russian, and he can speak with everyone, even with the lame chairman of the collective farm who drives a two-wheeled horse cart.

We can also speak Russian, 'cause as we still lived at home, we spoke one day German and the other day – Russian. We don't do like that here. We speak German with our mother and Russian – with father. And with neighbours we also speak only Russian, 'cause they don't understand German. But only Grandpa Semenych always laughs at me, when I speak Russian with him. He even mimics me, as if he were a child. But I don't hold anything against him. Then I start speaking German, and he doesn't understand anything. Then I also laugh at him. But he doesn't hold anything against me, neither. He says then,

"Agreed, Fedjka! I shan't be mocking at you anymore. Come on! So be it, tousle my beard!"

I like to tousle the beard of Grandpa Semenych; it is big, and I always find something in it, now and then: a grass-blade or a piece of thread. And once, I even got pricked, 'cause there was a tiny timber splinter there. Only I don't like when he calls me Fedjka. Then I tell him that my name is Fritzik, for a grown-up man it would be Fritz or Friedrich, as the name of my father is.

"When I'll grow up," I tell him, "I'll be called Friedrich Karlowich, like my father." But Grandpa Semenych is laughing then again.

Somebody is shouting out there in the street. I'm peeking out of the window.

"The carts are coming!" I jump off the tiny log.

Father is getting up. And Mother is also getting up. She tells me,

"Be in a hurry, Fritzik, put on your shoes."

Mother makes me hurry up. She even helps me.

Somebody's knocking at the door. Little Karl's father is coming in.

„Hello, everybody," he says, „Teacher, they are waiting for you."

All grown-ups call my father Teacher and address him with respect. And children from the school, where Arno learned, call my father Friedrich Karlowich. And the Russians call him Friedrich Karlowich. As I asked my mother, why the grown-ups call my father Teacher, she said that earlier at home all teachers were used to be addressed that way. That's why they say so, even now.

"And when it was earlier?" I asked.

"By the time I wasn't in the land of the living," Mother says.

"And when I wasn't in the land of the living?"

Mother can't explain it to me. Maybe, she doesn't know it, neither.

My father puts on his long coat. Mother uses to cover me and Arno with it for the night. Father takes his hat and pack, and comes up to the door. He looks round the whole room once more, as if he doesn't want to forget anything, looks at us and says,

"Well, let's go."

The street is filthy. There're several horse carts on the road. There are some men on them. They're looking at us. They're waiting for my father.

Women and children are standing around the carts. They're also looking at us.

My father is going along the pathway close to our house. There's clean sand on the pathway. My father has strewed it on it, so that we didn't walk in mud. The sand on the pathway is wet.

On the corner of the pathway father gets out of the pathway and steps straight into the soggy soil, 'cause the little Karl's father is heading to the horse carts, and my father clears the way for him.

Father doesn't want us to go further. He turns round to look at Arno and stretches out his hand to him. Arno also stretches out his hand, 'cause Arno's already grown-up and he's got a red tie.

"Well, son, goodbye," Father says, "Remember, we were talking about. Now, you are the only man in our house."

"I'll do everything," Arno says, without raising his head.

My father hugs Arno. He rather only presses Arno's head to his coat, just over the pocket. 'Cause even though Arno's grown-up, he's small, but father is so-o tall. Father stands quite upright; he's only tilted his head. He's grooming Arno's hair on the crown, and then puts his hand on brother's shoulder.

"Goodbye," he says, "I rely on you."

Arno looks down and nods his head. He goes away from father. There're tears in his eyes. He turns aside from me, but all the same, I've seen it. And I'll be teasing him in the evening, shame on him, such a grown-up already and cries.

And Maria, as well. Even before she came to Father, she started to howl and wasn't in any way ashamed of it; and soon she'll go to school, you know. Whoopee! They'll catch it from me to-day!

Father kisses her right in the wet cheek.

Now he turns to me. Mother shoves me to him. I'm walking straight into his stretched arms. My father lifts me up high into the sky, so that his face is in front of me.

"Embrace me, Sonny," Father says softly.

I like to hug Father. I put my arms around his neck and pull it to myself, with all might I have. Father's chin is a bit prickly, and I like it. I don't let it off and wait till Father says, "Ooh- ooh, let me off, or else you'd throttle me fully!"

But now, Father says nothing. Maybe, I've throttled him to death already? I let him off and look at him, whether he's alive or not. Two tears are rolling down on his cheeks. Maybe, these're the tears of Marijke. At first, they're big, and then they're rolling down and are getting smaller. It's so, 'cause they've left glittering tracks on the cheeks. As these tracks nearly reach the mouth, the tears are quickly moving to different sides: Father's got two deep wrinkles round his mouth, and the tears can't get out of them, in no way.

I smooth out with my finger one of the wrinkles. One of the tears comes up to my finger. I'm making a track with my finger right downwards, and the tear is also following this track right downwards like a raindrop on the window pane, when it's cold out there, but warm indoors.

Father kisses me on both cheeks. I don't like to be kissed, I'm not a little girl, you know. I'll be a Red Army commander, as my grandpa was, you know. I'm wiping dry with my small palm my cheeks and say,

"Father, bring me a little camel, the silvery one that could be hanged on a Christmas tree."

But Father doesn't say anything. He only presses me to himself, so that I nearly give a yell. Maybe, Father hasn't heard me?

"Such a camelly that Marijke has lost, Father."

"All right, Sonny, agreed," Father says it very gently again.

But he says it like our grandma, when she didn't want that I bothered her. One wouldn't say so about a silvery camelly.

"The one with two humpettes…" I show it with my bended small hands.

Father's putting me down on the ground.

Mother's coming up to him. That's it, she's also crying. But not so loud, to tell the truth. Otherwise, they could hear it, out there on the road, and then she'll be ashamed of it. She's nestled with her face amongst his breast, embraced him and she's caressing the back of his coat. Maybe, she's pitting the coat, 'cause there'll be nothing to cover me and Arno with for the night.

"It's about time," Father says and moves Mother a little bit aside. "Don't worry. Everything will be all right. We'll prove that it's not so," he says, "By all means. It's necessary. At least for them," Father nods with his head to the side, where I'm standing with Marijke and Arno. He's looking once more at us, "It's about time. Goodbye."

Father is going to the carts with brisk steps.

There're already plenty of people there. But more and more aunties and uncles are coming out of the courtyards. Maybe, they'll be following the horse carts till the limits of the village. I also want to go along with the horse carts till the village limits but I'm not allowed to do that. We stay standing by our house and are looking at the road.

Our father has got onto the horse cart there. The horse carts have moved off. Everyone has followed them. Many of them are crying, but we are waving goodbye to our father. But father isn't looking our way and then he isn't seen anymore.

The next day I go out. I've put on my mitten, 'cause it's got cold. There's ice instead of puddles everywhere today. The ice is thin and white, and if you strike it with the heel, it gets broken, and it turns out that there is nothing under it. Where's the water got to? It couldn't get upwards, there's ice there, you know. But at the bottom, the earth is frozen-stiff and it wouldn't let the water through. I can't even make small holes in earth with a small nail I have.

The whole of the road is uneven and rough. After the horse carts drove on it, everything got hardened. It's better not to walk on it. You'd stumble along all the time.

I'm going home. Near the corner of the house I notice a big footstep. It's the father's footstep! My father stood here yesterday! The footstep has stiffened from the frost and looks as if my father has just left the place. I'm carefully

Illustration by Swetlana Hinz

putting my boot into Father's footstep and check, whether it's got quite frozen. The footstep is stiff.

I'm running home. I tell no one about the footprint. I only fear that it would melt. In the evening I ask Mother,

"Wouldn't it be warm tomorrow?"

"May be not, Sonny," Mother says, "The gusts of wind are pretty cold today. Don't go out today to no purpose."

I don't go out without a need. It's really very cold out there all the time. I go out only to have a look at Father's footprint. The Father's footstep has got frozen stiff and inside there's a white line at its rim. Maybe, someone drew it with a piece of chalk there? I know, what chalk is. Chalk looks like a piece of bar, you can write with it at school. When we still lived at home we had chalk, and Marijke wrote letters with it for me on the porch. Marijke can write letters. Our father has taught her. He also took her to school with him.

One day, Marijke covered with letters the whole of the porch. Then our mother came out and said that she should stop writing and letters had to be scratched off from all wooden planks. Marijke wetted a rag and began to scratch off the letters from all those planks. I told her that Mother said to scratch them off only from one plank, not from all of them, but Marijke told me that the whole of the porch was a chalkboard. She scratched off all the letters, but nevertheless they could be seen a little bit. She had to clean and wash the porch.

I'm touching with the tip of my finger the white line in Father's footstep. Black ground is peeping out under my finger and the fingertip is getting wet. No, it's may be not a chalk. I'll be not scratching off the whole of the line. Let it be so, it does look more beautiful so.

It is frosty outdoors. Maybe, the footstep is feeling cold. I tear out a bundle of straw from the barn's roof and blanket the Father's footstep. Next morning, there's no straw on the footstep. It's the wind that's puffed it away.

I've spotted an old piece of rag in the barn. I shake the dust out of it and stretch it over the Father's footstep. I lay stones over the edges of the rag, so that the wind wouldn't puff it away. Now it would be warm for the Father's footstep.

Mother asks in the evening, "Who has brought so many stones under the window?" I say, „That's been me, I play there."

The snow fell down during the night. It's also covered the rag. I take away the stones, shake off the snow and make again the bed for the Father's footstep.

Mother says in the evening,

"Thank goodness! It's snowing. Let it be heavy snow, or else the whole of the earth would get deep-frozen."

"Would it be really warm for it under the snow?" I ask.

"Under the snow it'll be warm for it," Mother says.

I don't understand how it could be warm under the cold snow. But as Mother says so, then it may be true. Before, mother also said things, which I couldn't understand, but later, when I checked it up, it turned out to be so, as Mother said.

I'm not shaking off the snow from the rag anymore. I let very much snow drift over the Father's footstep, so that it would be warm for it.

Mother is at work. Arno's also at work – he's sledging beet-roots from the field. All grownup boys from our village are sledging beetroots from the field.

The beetroots in the field have been heaped up in a big pile that is as large as our house. The whole of the pile has been drifted by snow, and it's turned into a snow mountain. Hares would come running to this mountain. They eat up the beetroots to the full, climb up the mountain, and slither down, then. Arno sees them every day.

I haven't seen these hares and don't know, how they sled from the mountain, 'cause they have neither a sledge nor an old sack you may sit on. May be they've got such bent planks, which Grandpa Semenych has. They call these planks skis, and Grandpa Semenych ties them to his felt boots. But Arno says that hares have got neither skis nor felt boots.

Each day Arno gets two big beetroots as a pay for his work. We bake the beetroots in the stove and then they are very, very tasty. One beetroot is enough for all of us to eat at one time.

For me and Marijke Mother leaves half a beetroot for lunch. We can't eat it all at once, but toward the evening we eat up the whole of it.

I've just had lunch with Marijke. She's sitting on the stove knitting a sock. Maybe, she's outstripped me far and away, by now. So be it. I've got tired of knitting. If these socks would be for us, I'd be also knitting them, but all the same Mother would bring them away to someone. I don't want to knit; I've got tired of it. My loin is aching, you know. Even in my sleep I'm knitting and knitting, and stitches continue to slide down the needles, and there're so many of them. In my dreams, they would keep on sliding down the whole night. And they don't let me gather them again. Then I shriek and wake up.

I don't know why, but Marijke says nothing to me. Maybe, she wants that I'd be not knitting as long as possible. Then she'd be the first to finish the sock.

Illustration by Swetlana Hinz

No, my loin isn't aching. I've only joked. Only the lazy ones say so. I'm not lazy. I've just wanted to play with someone a little bit, but there isn't anyone to play with. So be it. I only want to have a look through the window for a while, and then I'll be knitting again.

I'm breathing on the glass of the window till there appears a clear melted circle. I'm looking through this circle. There's a very, very huge snowdrift under the window. It has even covered a part of the window; its edge is dark underneath. Now, there might be very warm for the Father's footprint.

Everything is white outdoors, and the sun is shining very, very brightly. It's good that the circle on the window glass is small, and I can see only with one eye. 'Cause, if I'd see with two eyes at once maybe I'd go blind.

There isn't anyone to be seen outdoors. There's always no one to be seen there. All kids are whiling away their time at home.

I'm looking there, where Elsa lives. Somebody's going up the street. This is Auntie Dasha who brings letters. She's passing by the Elsa's house. She always goes to see only the houses, where Russians live. After that, some aunties would wear black shawls. Maybe, Auntie Dasha carries black shawls around? Maybe, the Russian fathers send them from the front.

I wish my father also sent a black shawl to my mother. The mother's shawl is quite old already.

Auntie Dasha has neared our house. She opens her bag, looks into it and goes straight to our house.

"Have you brought a black shawl for my mother?" I ask Auntie Dasha, as she comes in.

"What black shawl?" asks she, "I've brought a letter from your father. Dance!"

A letter from my father! May be he's also sent a camelly to me? This could be great!

Marijke's singing a merry German song and dancing. I'm jumping very, very high!

We don't open the letter. Let everyone come back home, then mother would read it aloud. We climb on the stove and carry on knitting. We want to finish the socks till mother comes. She'd praise us for our work and tomorrow would bring these socks to the village council, so that the village council could send them to the front. There, our Red Army soldiers and commanders would put the socks on, and it'd be warm for their feet, and they'd be able more quickly to go forward and to drive away the fascists. Then, the war will be over, and all fathers would come back to their children, and all people would be able again to live at home again.

Mother comes home together with Arno. Marijke wants mother also to dance, but she's not dancing. She only sits down on the bench, undoes the upper button of her coat, moves the shawl on to the back of her head and then she's sitting still, just so. But Arno's jumping up to the ceiling shouting, "Hurrah! Death to the fascist invaders!" And he's throwing his hat, mittens and scarf high in the air. Marijke and I start again jumping and shouting together with Arno.

Father doesn't write anything about the school. Neither has he written about the village he lives in. He only writes that he works in Taiga, his village may be called so. Also he writes that he's doing well and there're plenty of fir-trees there, and everything looks beautiful in winter, and that mother shouldn't worry about him, his work isn't a hard one. I can't remember what kind of work he has. Mother explains to me that he says in Russian what others say in German and then he says in German what others say in Russian. I can't see why my father by all means shouldn't speak the way the others speak. But mother says that it's needed, so that people could understand each other; then they'll be able to work well. And she adds that Father is having a good work, not cutting trees, thank goodness!

But Father doesn't write anything about a camelly. Maybe, he just wants to bring it with him, when he comes back. I'm telling Mother to write to him that he could send me a camelly. It's not needed to bring it with him. He may take it down from one of the Christmas trees. There're many fir-trees there, you know, and send the camelly with his letter.

But Mother says that the camelly would get creased and broken with the letter on its way. And it's true. The whole of Father's letter has got wrinkled. Agreed, let it be so, I'll wait till Father comes.

At night, I'm dreaming of Father's village Taiga. It's very, very big and there're big fir-trees in all the streets, and there're toys on all the fir-trees; they're glittering and sparkling. I'm walking with my father amidst the fir-trees and when I'm speaking German with him, he's answering in Russian, and if I'm speaking Russian, he's answering in German. It's an interesting play, I'm laughing, and Father's laughing, too. And I know now, why Father's saying everything the other way. It's to make it so that people had a lot of fun. And we are tearing off tiny silvery camels from the fir-trees. We're gathering very, very many of them, and when I don't have any place to stock more of them, they suddenly fall out of my hands straight on the white snow. I want to pick them up, but they aren't to be seen on the snow, not a bit. I'm telling my father about it, but Father is silent. I'm looking upwards. Father is looking at me stock-still. Two big tears are rolling down his cheeks. I'm showing my empty hands to my father, 'cause the camellies are unseen on the snow. But Father is only looking at me silently. Then he starts to float away somewhere, and he's floating away, and floating away, till he's entirely out of sight.

I want to have a look at the Father's footstep. But if I'd brush away the snow, it'd be cold for it. I'd better dig out a hole in the snowdrift, like the one the children next door have dug out in front of their house.

It's not handy to dig with the shovel. It's heavy, and its handle is thick. As soon as I gather enough snow on it, it would slip over in my hands, and all the snow would fall down from it. Then I take the pan that mother uses to melt snow when she means to wash her hair. It's better with the pan. I rake up snow in it and bring it aside.

Now I see the stones. I bring a brush, brush away all the snow from the rag and sweep out the hole, too. Then I open the Father's footstep. It's the same as I'd covered it before that.

Now I often come to see the father's footstep. It's really warmer in the hole than outside. As I go away I cover the entry with an old iron lid from the Russian stove and pour some snow over it.

Now Auntie Dasha goes and sees the German houses as well. She's also brought some black shawls to them already. But she brings only letters to us. Father always writes that he's doing the same work and that Mother doesn't have to worry. Then we don't have any letters for a very, very long time. By the time as almost all snow had melted down and the hole over the father's footstep fell in, Mother and Arno bring a strange uncle from the railway station. They take him from the horse-cart and bring him holding in their arms into the house. They say that he's my father. But he isn't my father. He's only called like my father - Friedrich Karlowich.

Friedrich Karlowich lies all the time in bed; my mother asked Grandpa Semenych for it. He can't get up at all. Neither can he sit – Mother puts pillows under his back and then it seems, as if he's sitting. His neck is thin and long, and his nose is also long, whereas the eyes are big and stare blankly, as if there isn't anything in front of them. At the point, where Father cheeks had, Friedrich Karlowich has deep hollows. His upper lip is short and he's always showing his teeth.

When I'm asking Mother, why Friedrich Karlowich is always showing his teeth, she says that its so, 'cause he's thin. I'm also thin, you know, Mother herself said it so, but I'm not showing my teeth, not at all.

Now, strange aunties come to us every evening. I don't know them. They question Friedrich Karlowich. Friedrich Karlowich can't speak very long. He'd say some words, and then he'd breathe heavily with his open mouth. Every evening he'd tell only one auntie about her husband. The aunties themselves have agreed on it so. But they'd come all of them. And they'd often cry. But they aren't crying as I and Marijke do. When we cry, then we cry with voice as well as with nose and eyes; whereas, aunties do cry only with their eyes.

Mother is also crying with them. She says,

„Just imagine it! He'd been cutting trees all this time. And he wrote home..."

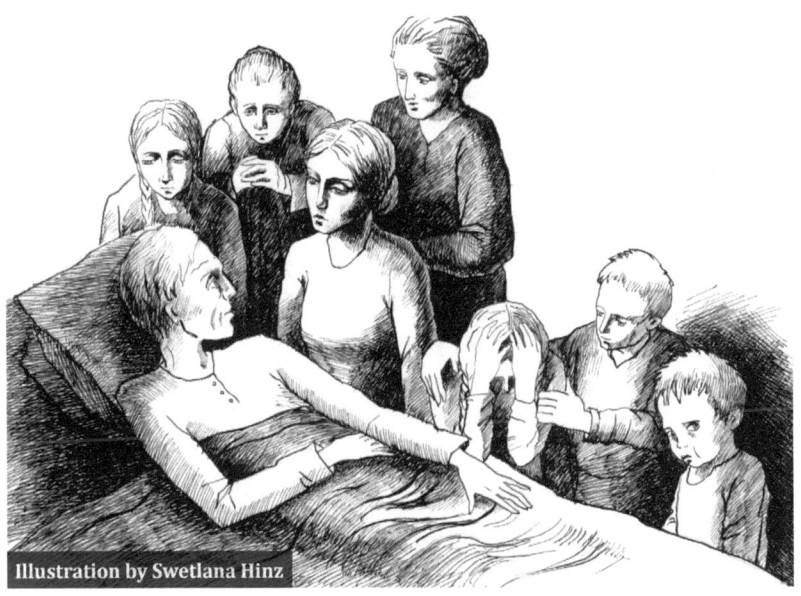

Illustration by Swetlana Hinz

Friedrich Karlowich would finish telling and then he'd be looking somewhere ahead very, very far away. Everyone would be looking at him, but he'd be silent and wouldn't move a bit. Only his left eye is jerking sometimes. It's 'cause he's got a deep scar over the eye. The scar is from the twig that fell down from the tree straight on his head. Friedrich Karlowich told the aunties so. But he didn't tell so to Mother as she asked him about the scar earlier. He told Mother quite otherwise, I've heard it myself.

"We were led to a party meeting..." he said then and breathed air, "I couldn't stand anymore, fell down... With a gun butt..."

Marijke has also begun to call Friedrich Karlowich as father. Maybe, she's forgot my father like Mother and Arno.

Once, as everyone has got out somewhere from the house, I come up to Friedrich Karlowich and ask him,

"Tell me; were there many toys on the fir-trees in your village?"

He shakes his head.

"Do you know, where the footstep of my father is?"

Sure, he doesn't know. He only turns to me his head and eyes that don't see me, 'cause they look so, as if they've been showered with a soft grey ash, and puts his hand on my head. His hand is like a piece of tree bark. I move aside and his hand falls down onto the bed.

If he were my father, he'd know, where his footstep is and that there're many toys on the fir-trees in that beautiful father's village Taiga.


At first Mother spoon-feeds Friedrich Karlowich. Then he's able to drink milk out of the glass by himself. He always asks for more, but mother gives him only half a glass of it.

Grandma of Grandpa Semenych has brought a crock with cream in it for us. She's never lived at home, where we lived, with her grandpa. They've always been living here, in this village, that's why they haven't left their cow home. Their cow is called Zorka.

Mother puts the crock under the bench and tells us that it's only for Father. But she gives cream to drink only to Friedrich Karlowich. She gives also only half a glass of cream to him. He drinks looking at the crock, and his whole body starts trembling.

"Ah, Fritz, you shouldn't so much," Mother says, "Be patient just for several days more."

Today is my turn not to lie beside Mother in bed. I'm lying by the side of the bed. Marijke is lying to the right of me, then Mother, and then Arno.

Among us only Marijke doesn't lie by the side of the bed, 'cause she's a girl, you know, and she'd never be a Red Army commander.

Now Marijke is now lying close beside me. She's pulled her legs to her belly, embraced the Mother's arm, nestled her nose against the Mother's shoulder, and she's snuffling. I've embraced Marijke and nestled against her neck. Marijke's buttock is warm, and her whole body is warm, that's why I'm also warm. Only there's a draught from behind. Maybe, Arno's pulled the blanket to himself, 'cause there's a draught from the window there. I'm trying to drag the blanket to myself, but it wouldn't go. Then I turn with my back to Marijke, so that my back could also be warmed up a little bit. Marijke's buttock moves back from me right away. Now, there's more place under the blanket, I cover myself and crawl near to Marijke again. She's turning over and squealing for a bit, but she hasn't got place anymore to move anywhere and gets quite. I'm warm now and fall asleep.

In my sleep I see two dreams. At first, I see a dream about Father. It's a somewhat dark dream. May be, 'cause Father is far away.

The dream about Father hasn't been over yet, as began a dream about Friedrich Karlowich. This dream is a bright one, 'cause when Mother goes to bed, she takes away the stool from the window, and everything is seen in the room.

I'm lying on the floor by the bed of Friedrich Karlowich. Friedrich Karlowich comes down from the bed, goes down on all fours and is creeping along past me. He's leaning with his arm on my leg, but I don't feel pain, and he doesn't notice it, anyway. He crawls up to the bench, sits down on the floor, takes the crock with cream, and drinks. He's drinking very long, the crock is shaking in his hands, and cream is dropping on his shirt. Then he goes down on all fours again and crawls back. When he's crawling past me, he's breathing heavily and beads of sweat glitter on his face. Maybe, he's very tired. It seems to be above his strength, he can't even walk, you know, and the crock is very heavy. Even for me it's too heavy to lift it.

"Is it really heavy?" I ask whispering. But he doesn't say anything. He isn't even looking at me. He's climbing up onto the bed again.

I wake up, 'cause Mother's crying loudly. I ask Arno, why Mother's crying. Arno says that Friedrich Karlowich is dead.

Then, many people come to us. They've come to bury Friedrich Karlowich. To bury means to bring to the small hill beyond the village and to lay him in the sun. It's warm there and birds are singing. I want also to be buried till night, but

Arno says that it's muddy to go there, and my boots are worn out. Arno brings me to Grandpa Semenych. I could have walked myself, as far as his house; however Zorka's standing by the barn. Zorka's given to butting with her horns, and I'm afraid of her.

Zorka rubs against corners. We also had a cow at home. In spring, she was also rubbing against corners. They shed their hair so. At that time, Arno gathered the old hair and rolled up a ball out of it. He then played that ball with kids in the street.

"Arno," I say, "Look, Zorka's shedding her hair. Would you roll up a ball out of it for me?"

"Agreed," Arno says, "I'll roll it up".

Arno's good. I like him.

In the evening, Arno takes me up. We're going home. I stop by the corner of the house, where there was the Father's footstep. Arno also stops.

There's no father's footstep anymore. There're plenty of trails from cows' hoofs.

The red hair shreds are stuck in the black cracked butt-ends of house logs.

"Arno," I say, "let's gather this hair."

Arno doesn't say anything. He takes me by the hand and leads home.

It's cold in our house. Mother has undone her coat and she's sitting at the table and just looking in front of her; she's silent. Marijke's climbed up onto the stove, wrapped herself up, and she's also silent. Arno's brought the firewood from the porch, took a dry log from behind the stove and is chipping thin splinters to light the stove. Neither is he saying anything. That means I also have to be silent and not to bother anyone.

I don't undress; I only take off my boots and climb up onto the bed, where Friedrich Karlowich lay. The linen has been already taken from the bed, and I'm walking on the planks as if on the floor. A small shelf is hanging in the room's corner over the bed. All sorts of papers are lying on the shelf; Mother calls them "documents". I and Marijke aren't allowed to touch them.

There're also various photos on the shelf. Most of them are with my father sitting in the middle, and there're very, very many children all around him. We are allowed to touch the photos. I like to look at photos.

I sit down on the bed and sort out all the photos; those with children – to the right. It turns out to be very, very many children. I didn't even know before that there're so many children in the world. I wonder only, where they all have gone away. In our village there wouldn't be enough children even for one such photo.

Then I take from the shelf other photos. They're without children; there're only uncles and aunties on them. These photos I place to the left of me. So, I get very, very many people around me.

I know many of them.

This uncle with a round little thing with a chainlet on the soldier's blouse is uncle Willi. He's my father's brother. He's fighting at the front. Once we've even got a letter from him from there. And not long ago we got a letter from him again. He wrote that all of them, who stayed alive, had been gathered from the front and sent to Taiga. Friedrich Karlowich said, as mother showed him the letter, that though it was far away from him, it was all the same, all in all. Uncle Willi is smiling in the photo.

And this uncle, who's sitting on the stool with a saber, is my mother's uncle. He was a soldier of Budyonny's army. These

Budyonny's soldiers are the people who were galloping on horseback with a red flag and were fighting with the Whites. Each of them has a red flag in one hand and a saber – in the other. And who are the Whites I don't know. I know only that they had killed many people there, where Father and Mother lived as we were still at home, and I wasn't among the livings, yet. They also killed the Mother's uncle. They fully cut off his head. That's why when he was buried, at first he was put in a coffin, and then – his head.

And this is my own grandpa. 'Cause he's Father's father. He's also with a saber and a handgun, only on horseback. My grandpa was a commander. He had a full unit of soldiers, and all of them were on horseback. My grandpa was fighting with Vakulin who was riding around with his band.

Grandma often told Grandpa, "You'd better give it up, Vakulin would get you, and it'll be very bad for you". But my grandpa was only laughing and repeating, "Wait a bit, mother; I'll get him myself someday."

And then Vakulin came at night to the village and closed a ring round my grandpa. In the morning he rounded up the whole village to the church and hung up my grandpa with a rope round his neck. Grandpa hung the whole day, he couldn't breathe and died 'cause of that. Only in the evening they cut the rope and took down Grandpa.

I like to see these photos. I only don't like, when Mother tells somebody about them. I then shut my ears very tightly so that I wouldn't hear anything and I'm looking at Mother's lips and waiting till she starts telling something else. I'm very scared to listen to it; I always dream after it that my head is also cut off with a smooth chilly saber. I don't feel pain, I'm only scared that my head would be apart from me and that after this, maybe, I'd be dead.

My grandpa is lifelike in the photo. He looks like my father, and I'm looking at him very, very long. I love him. I often see him in my sleep. He's seating me ahead of him on his horse; and we're riding very, very high above the earth, I'm holding upwards a red flag, and Grandpa – a saber...

And we've got one more photo with a tractor. The tractor goes up the street, and there're very, very many people around, and kids are running in front of it.

And we've also got a photo with many uncles and aunties planting small thin trees.

Once more I've a look at all photos that are laid out around me, then collect them and put them on the shelf.

But, what is this booklet about? It's quite small and thin. It wasn't here before.

I open the booklet. There's also a small photo in it, only it's glued to the booklet. But this is my father, really! My Paapa... He's looking straight at me! He's looking so, as if he's trying very much to look very strict, but all the same it's seen that he's kind. He looked that way when Mother used to tell him, "Our Fritzik, Papa, wasn't a very much obedient child today, you know". Father then made such a strict face and said, "Aa-nd? And what's the matter Fritzik? Now then, come here; let's talk as man to man."

I liked it, when Father talked to me as man to man. He seated me beside him on the stool; and his eyes were very, very kind and I was telling him very, very honestly about everything. He'd never scolded me. And I understood everything! And he used to tell me after that,

"So be it, I only beg you to remember that Mother shouldn't be disappointed; the matter is..." he'd bend down to me and say very quietly so that only I could hear, "The matter is that you and I should be very much considerate

towards women, 'cause they are really weak, not the sort as we men are. Agreed?"

I fully agreed with my father. And after talking to him I became almost as big and strong as he was. Only my height was small. And then Father was telling me,

"Well, I'm glad that both of us do think the same way. It's always pleasant to have like-minded persons, you know... And now you can smother me a little bit."

I put my arms around Father's neck and smothered him with all my might. After that he didn't try to do his face as strict as in the photo...

I jump off the bed,

"Mummy! Look, my Papa!"

Mother starts, turns to me and takes the booklet.

"It's the father's party membership card, Sonny," she says.

"And what does this party card mean?" I ask.

"Your father was a communist," Mother says.

But all the same I don't understand it.

"And who are these communists?" I ask.

Mother thinks about it. Then she says,

"Communists are those people who want that all the working people in the world had a good living."

Now I'm thinking about it. I'm thinking about the early time as we lived at home; and we lived well then – everybody says so, you know.

"Mum, but as we lived at home, we were working people, weren't we?"

"Certainly, my little Sonny, we were."

Then, that's right. We were working people and we lived well. But why do we live so badly, now? Maybe, we aren't working people anymore, are we?

"Mama, and are we the working people now?

"And now, as well," Mother says.

A can't understand it again. I'm thinking for some time about it, but all the same I don't catch it.

"And are we still living in the World?" I ask.

Mother is looking at me so, as if she can't understand something.

"Yeh, sure, where else then?" she answers slowly, turns to me her whole head and starts looking at me as if I'm seriously ill. Then all of a sudden she clasps my head to her bosom and warm drops one by one are falling down on the top of my head.

# 2. Mother

It's grown completely dark and it's been getting cold already. Maybe, it's got already quite cold down there in the room.

Marijke and I are lying on the stove. The stove's still a little bit warm. We've wrapped ourselves up in a blanket and are reckoning what mother and Arno would bring.

"They'd bring today bread," I say, "such a piece."

I want bread very much. Mather hasn't brought any since very, very long.

"No one is having bread now," she says.

Yesterday, they brought five boiled potatoes and a bowl of thick potato peelings. When Arno comes home, we'll bake the peelings in the stove. If baked, they're very, very tasty. Almost all of their husk would be then burnt out, and if you'd rub a little bit with finger, only the white would be left.

And it'd be also wonderful, if some auntie would get a letter from Taiga. As Auntie Berta the other day. She came to us, as Friedrich Karlowich had been buried already, and brought half a pan of oatmeal.

„Take... for your children..." Auntie Berta said, held out the pan to Mama and started to whine, "My younger has sent a letter... he was quite weak, lost weight... couldn't do the

job norm anymore... ration got smaller... the teacher used to give him from his bread... saved him... Ewald was his pupil, you know...“

Mother was whining a long time then and couldn't calm herself down in any way. Auntie Berta had even to give her a glass of water. Then Mother put the pan on the table, and we all started to eat the oatmeal. And Mother made also Auntie Berta to eat with us. The oatmeal was indeed tastier than the baked potato peelings.

Yeh, it'd be good if Mother and Arno could bring some bread. Maybe, someone would have it today and they'd give it to them?

"No, they won't bring bread. No one is having bread now," Marijke repeats the Mother's saying.

"And was it before?"

"Before, everyone had it," Marijke says, "All my girl-friends had bread at home. As I played for a long time at theirs, we were given a piece of bread. And when we played at ours mother gave it, too. That bread was very, very white and soft; and its crackling was such... you know, the one that crunches. Mother used to spread bread with butter and strew some sugar on it. It's so tasty, you know!..“ „And with salt it's also tasty," Marijke adds.

"And everyone had bread?" I ask.

"Everyone had," Marijke says.

I like it, when Marijke tells about our house. She's lucky, Mother bought her earlier and she ate bread with butter, as much as she wanted. And I was bought, when nobody had bread already. Not even a brown one.

But maybe, Marijke thinks it all up? How could it be that everyone has bread?! Where they get it all from? And even the white one. And with butter. And with sugar...

Sure, she thinks it all up... But let her think up. All the same, it's interesting.

„And everyone had fathers at home?" I ask Marijke.

"Everyone had," she answers and starts whining then.

"Why are you whining?" I ask her.

She's goes on whining a little bit and says then,

"Don't ask me about Father, I'm getting upset 'cause of that."

"Agreed, I won't do that... I want to eat. And it's cold. Maybe, we'll light the stove?" I say.

"No, Mother didn't allow it."

"And if they won't come today?"

Marijke's silent. Then she says,

"They'll come. They always come, you know. Only we shouldn't forget to tell that Auntie Ida was here."

We are silent. Why Mother has been called to the village administration? There's no work now. And Mother can't work. She's ill. Something is aching in her tummy...

It's calm. The snow's creaking somewhere in the street. The creak is nearing. Somebody knocks on the door. We jump off the stove, Marijke runs to open the door, and I peep out into the tiny porch. That's Mother and Arno, they've come. Marijke's brushing off the snow from their felt boots.

Mother puts a small bag on the table, takes off the mittens, and unwinds the shawl.

"Undo my coat, Fritzik," she says, and sits down on the bench.

I undo her coat. Then I take her cold hands and put them on my head.

„Warm them up," I say.

My hair is long. Mother plants her hands in it and rubs them against my hair.

Her hands are stark and stiff.

"Hold them tightly," I say and start very, very fast to turn my head from left to right, back and forth, so that even my head is spinning.

"Are they warm now?" I ask.

"They're, thank you," Mother says smoothing my hair down.

She goes to the stove, opens the damper, and rakes through a little heap of ashes. There's still a small piece of smoldering coal there. Thank goodness, otherwise we'd have to run to Grandpa Semenych and ask him for some cinder. Mother blows out this smoldering piece of coal and lights a thin long splinter of dry wood. It's getting light in the room.

Now Arno will quickly kindle the stove, boil some water, and we'll be dining.

We want to see what Mother and Arno have brought. But it's not allowed to steal into this small bag on the table. It's bad to do it. We should wait, till all of us would sit down at table and Mother would pour out boiled water into small clay pots. Arno's brought these clay pots from the forest. They've been hanged up there on trees so that the pine resin flew down into them. It's very tasty to drink boiled water from them. You wouldn't get your lips burnt and it's not hot for hands. When Mother would pour out boiled water, she'd turn over her small bag and would empty out everything onto the table.

Now we're at the table. Now there're two boiled potatoes in mother's bag for each of us and one more is left there. The potatoes are cold and mushy. They've rolled in the bag and all sorts of chunk have stuck to it. We brush away the chunks and strew coarse salt on it. Tasty! There's also a piece of baked pumpkin in this tiny bag.

"They've given it to me!" Arno says pointing to the pump-kin, "A good auntie came across. She says, 'Sit down, and eat a piece.' I say, 'No, I've got one more sister and a brother at home, I can't.' She says, 'Well, all the same, sit down. If you'll eat it, I'll give you one more piece, you'll bring it home. I wanted, Mum, to hide half a piece for you, but she noticed. She says, 'If you wouldn't eat, I wouldn't give...'"

"It's all right, Sonny." Mother says, "They also gave me to eat there, where I'd altered a dress..."

"And in another house a very angry uncle came across. 'You,' he says, 'don't speak correct Russian. Who are you?' I say, ,German.' And he, ,German? And you're begging yet that I gave you something? Let the fascists give you! Go out of here, you cub, while you're safe and sound!' And drove me out! I even couldn't tell him that I'm a different German, that I'm a Soviet pioneer."

Arno sniffed with his nose.

"Calm down, Sonny. Different people come across, you know. All the same, the good ones are in the majority."

"I'm ashamed, Mum. I'm really trying to say everything in correct Russian, but they make out anyway that I'm a German."

"That's not for you, Sonny. You speak very well. If only I could so..."

We're dipping potatoes into a cloth with salt and listening to Mother and Arno.

"Ouch, I've nearly forgotten," Marijke says suddenly, "Mum, Auntie Ida was here, told us to tell you that tomorrow morning all of you must come to the village administration; it's very, very urgent."

"And why we're summoned, didn't she tell that?"

"No she didn't. She also doesn't know." Mother is ponder-ing for quite a while and sighs.

"Well, let's go to bed now," she says.

We're spreading the coat on the floor and dragging down the blanket from the stove. The stove hasn't warmed up enough, yet. It's chilly in the room and I don't want to kneel down to pray. To pray that means to say something to God. Before we didn't pray, but now we pray. It was the Grandma of Semenych who advised Mother to do it. She said,

"It doesn't matter that you don't believe. All the same, you pray. Anyway, it's as a kind of support. And without any, it's difficult to stand firm. It'll be shaking and rocking you and then you'll be knocked over. No-o, it's really necessary to believe in something."

"But in what else?" mother said, "There isn't anything left to believe in, you know…"

As the Grandma of Semenych had left, the Volodya's Grandma Louise who was also at our place, told my mother,

„Wise old woman… In my old age it's too late to begin once more, but for them," she nodded her head in my and Marijke's direction, "It really might be useful.

After a few days she brought some bits of paper covered with writing, and Mother has taught us to pray. And then Mother began also to pray. But she did it alone, after the rest of us had done it.

It's good to pray. When I pray to the Kind God, I forget everything what's happened during the day and begin to think, "What good things the Kind God will do for us tomorrow?" And the whole night I sleep, and wait, and I'm happy.

Only I don't want to kneel down, if it's cold. Earlier, when it was cold, we said prayers under a blanket in bed. But now, Mother is strict. She watches that we prayed well. "If you'd be standing on your kneels," Mother says, "then God would hear your prayers better."

I'm the first to say prayers – 'cause I'm the little one and my prayer is also the shortest one:

*"I'm a small little child,*
*my strength is frail.*
*I'd like very much to be blessed,*
*but don't know how this could be done.*
*Amen."*

The prayers of Marijke and Arno are longer. I've also learnt them already by heart.

Mother says prayers longer than all of us do. I'm already falling asleep, but she's still standing on her knees whispering something, and she's begging the Kind God for something.

Marijke's sitting at the table and painting with our red pencil the courtyard we had at home. We've got only one pencil, it was the Father's pencil, and everything turns out to be red in Marijke's paintings: the courtyard, our cow Meta, and the sun, and the trees. Now she's painting the water well in the courtyard. And then she'll be painting herself standing on the porch with a piece of bread. I know it already. She always paints it so.

The door is creaking in our tiny porch. That's Mother who's come.

"Well, what was there?" asks Arno who's baking potato peelings for us.

"Nothing special, just a meeting", Mother says wiping out her eyes. Her eyes are red. We're looking at her. Mother notices that we're looking at her.

"It's windy out there..." she says, "It's blowing just in the eyes; I've rubbed them sore so that they're even aching."

Arno gathers a handful of baked potato peelings.

"It's for Mother, agreed?" he tells us quietly.

"Agreed," we approve.

Arno brings the peelings to the table.

"They're tasty, Mum," he says, "try them."

Mother's eating the peelings and seems to be looking at something far away. Then she tells me and Marijke,

"Go out and have some fresh air for a while."

"But it's may be cold out there, it's windy, you know," Marijke says.

"It's not that bad, the wind is quite weak. Go out and have a walk."

And really, there isn't much wind out in the street. But it's cold. We begin to freeze up very soon and run back home. Arno's sitting and whining. Mother's soothing him.

„Arno, are you whining?" I ask.

Arno doesn't answer. Mother answers,

"I have to go to the rayon's center for a couple of days; that's why Arno's so upset. But I'll come back very soon."

"But why to the rayon's center?" Marijke asks.

"No idea, we've been just ordered."

"But why ordered?"

"But no… not that… Your eyes are wet already… I'll come back, come back soon, by all means!…"

But at that point Mother starts crying very, very loud, and we all are echoing her…

Auntie Ida with her little Heinz comes to us in the evening. They've come just so, to visit us.

We're playing with Heinzik. Hainzik's father would never return, he's been buried for good in the village Taiga. Auntie Ida and mother are talking. Auntie Ida says, "Let it be so. The chairman said that they'll be brought to the orphanage. Maybe, that would be even better."

And then she tells Mother something else, "You're lucky. You won't be taken. You'll stay with yours."

"Oh, no!" Mother says, "Everyone is taken now. Ill or not, they aren't taking that into account. It's not that time. You yourself have heard what they said in the village administration."

"Don't say that," Auntie Ida looks so, as if she's angry with Mother 'cause she's ill. And she even starts speaking louder, "You'll stay at home."

"For God's sake, Ida, stop it," Mother says pointing with her eyes at us.

"Why should I stop it!" Auntie Ida seems to be angry with Mother, "Let's bet: if you stay, you'll give me your felt boots and take mine."

"That's enough of your talking," Mother's also getting angry. Maybe, she doesn't want to swap her felt boots, which she has sewed on, for the trod down felt boots of Auntie Ida: gaily colored tagrags are sticking out through their holes.

"I'd give everything for only to stay."

"Then settled," says Auntie Ida rejoicing, "I reckon, the felt boots are mine."

Marijke's sleeping already now, Arno's also sleeping. But I can't fall asleep. Mama's standing on her knees and she's praying very, very long today.

Early in the morning they bring two round loaves of bread to us. It's for Mother from the village administration, they say. Mother wraps up one loaf in a white cloth and puts it on the shelf near the dishes.

"It's for you," Mother says, "Arno, you'd portion it for four days. You'd give a small piece a day to everyone.

Then Mother is looking at the second loaf, takes a knife and cuts a piece from it. The rest she puts in her small bag. This piece she divides once more into four.

Bread is soft and the knife is sharp; that's why there're almost no crumbs. There's only a brown dust on the table from the crisp crest of bread.

"Is this for the little mice?" I and Marijke ask.

"Let's give them to the mice. Maybe, they're also hungry," Mother says.

I and Marijke gather the bread dust in a heap, divide it into halves and bring it to the stove. There're two little holes there in the floor. If it's quiet in the room, the mice are going out of them. Each of us has his own little mouse. We pour out the bread dust to our mice and sit down at table. Now, everyone in our house would be having breakfast.

The village administration is very good anyway, you know. It's given us bread. But maybe, the Kind God has sent it to us? He's heard that we're praying well and told the village administration, "These children are good children, give them bread ..." So we mustn't be lazy to pray on our knees!

"You shouldn't eat so fast." Marijke tells me, "It isn't tasty so. You should pinch a little bit from the whole this way, put it in your mouth and suck. Then it'll be tasty and last long."

And really, almost nothing has remained of my little piece, and Marijke still has half of hers. I'm trying to do the way she's doing, but I can't.

"I can't do it this way," I say.

"Don't be greedy, don't gulp it down all at once; then you'll get it."

I'm trying once more, but the little tasty piece slides to the throat, on its own.

"I've swallowed it again," I say. Only a wee bit is left from the bread crust.

"Don't be upset, my little one," Mother says, "All in all, the bread is in your tummy."

Somebody's crying out there in the street. Mother startles. She straightens herself up and begins to dress quickly.

"Mama, but you won't go away forever, will you?" I ask.

"I won't, my little one, I'll be back soon. As soon as you eat up the bread I'll come back then."

Father also said that he'd be back soon, but he hasn't returned as yet. But maybe, Mother will go to Father and they'd come back then together?

"Would you go to Father?" I ask.

Mother gets down on the bench. Tears are falling on the dark cracked button of her coat. They are dropping down and breaking up into many tiny splashes. One drop gets into my eye. There's something that starts prickling in my eyes.

There in the street, someone shouts summoning people. Mother pulls me and Marijke to herself, Arno's also hugging mother. We're whining.

Somebody's knocking at the porch door. It opens and a strange grandpa wearing a sheepskin coat comes in. He's got a whip in his hand.

"Go ahead, Petrovna, be quick about it," he says, "Oh no, not that, here's the same..." he's clasping his sides with long coat sleeves. Mother starts crying even louder. "Well, stop burying yourself, that's enough. Go ahead, Petrovna, let's go. We've got to go." He's listening to us for just a little while more, then shouts angrily, "That's enough, get ready quickly! You think, we'd be waiting for you? On foot you'll be going

then! Quickly! If we come late to the rayon's center, we'll be dressed down! The rayon's chief would be very much angry! Be quick!"

Mother stands up.

"Children, don't forget to pray." she says, "Don't close the stove chimney early... Don't go out to no purpose..."

Mother always says so, when she goes out. Maybe, she's really leaving not for long.

"That's it, let's go, let's go," the grandpa takes her by the sleeve, "But the luggage you've forgot..." The grandpa takes the mother's pouch, "Well, well, well, and this one has taken only one loaf of bread with. Are you going to a birthday party? You've really been told, you know: the ration is for ten days. Only in the rayon's center you'll be staying for three days, and where you'll be brought after that who knows..." the grandpa is grumbling, "Now go out, move, we should have been already on the way long ago, anyway."

Mother goes out. We're quickly putting on our tiny coats and running after her. There're several horse sleighs on the road. We see how Mother's getting on the last horse sleigh and turning her back on our house.

The grandpa shouts out,

„Gee up! Go ahead!..."

There ahead, the whips began to crack and the snow to creak. The first horses are running already. Steam jets from their nostrils, covered with icicles, hit the road. Now the last horse has pulled off its sleigh.

"Ma-ma!" I and Marijke are shouting.

Mother turns back. She sees us; wants to jump off the sleigh, but other aunties are holding her tight. We're running to the road. The sleighs are already far away ahead. Two deep even lines are left after them on the snowed road.

The lines are getting longer and closer and closer to each other. From the horse cart that had brought our father away from us back then, there were also two lines left. But they weren't as even and beautiful...

Horses, carts and mother are getting somewhere downwards. Only a shaft bow of the horse harness is yet to be seen. A whip got up above it and fell down then.

Robert and Arthur come to us after two days. They're Arno's friends. They work together and go for firewood in the forest. Their mothers have also left for rayon's center. They've been also left with the little ones. Arthur has two and Robert three of them. Robert and Arthur want that we all move to one house and live together. So, they say, we'll be having a joyful time together and would need less firewood.

Arno agrees with them. We're also happy: we'd be not staying the whole day alone, but we'd be playing with other kids. We'd be playing blind man's bluff, five pebbles and we'd be also spinning buttons on a thread so hefty that they'd be buzzing.

We pack up our belongings, prop the door with a stick and go together to Robert, his little house is the biggest one.

We've eaten up the whole of our bread but Mother hasn't come back, as of yet.

I wanted that we ate it up as quickly as possible, since Mother told us that she'd return as soon as we eat up the whole of the bread. But Arno said that Mother ordered to ration bread for four days. If we wouldn't obey Mother, she may not come back 'cause of that.

We have nothing left to eat. Neither have Arthur and Robert. We haven't eaten today. Arno, Robert and Arthur went somewhere in the morning. All seven of us have climbed up onto the stove. We've been told to sleep a little bit at lunchtime; so we wouldn't want to eat. We've slept a little bit and now we're telling each other what we've dreamt of. All of us have seen the same dream: mothers have come back and brought us bread. We've already told about our dreams. Otto and Elsa who're smaller than I am began to whine. Bit by bit, we also start whining. Mother said that if someone is grief-stricken and he'd whine, it'd be easier for him afterwards. And it's really so, after we've whined we aren't as hungry as before. We start playing blind man's bluff.

When it's getting dark, Arno, Robert and Arthur come. They bring potatoes. We haven't eaten today anything, that's why two potatoes for each are laid in the pot.

After supper everyone says, "Thank you God for our daily bread. Amen."

Robert says that today we also must thank the head of the collective farm. That was he who took them to his house, came down into his cellar and gave them a bucket with potatoes. We're saying in chorus, "Thank you the head of the collective farm for our daily bread. Amen."

After two days somebody's is knocking at night. Robert comes to the door; Arno and Arthur take their small axes, which they have when they go into the forest, and stand next to him. All of us have woken up and we're looking at them. We're scared.

"Who's there?" Robert asks.

"Robert, is that you?" can be heard from behind the door.

"That's me."

"And are mine here?"

"Who's there?"

"Arno's mama. Open quickly."

"Ma-ma!" I and Marijke start crying and we're running to the door, "Ma-ma!"

The others probably think their mothers have come too. They're also jumping up and crying,

"Ma-ma!"

The door opens. Our mother is coming in. We don't recognize her at first; she's dressed in someone else's clothing. She enters the room and gets down to the floor. I fall on her neck – my mother has come! I'm kissing her cold cheeks, nose, and lips. Marijke wants to push me aside, but I've clutched at Mother's shawl and don't let her off.

"And where's our mother?" Elsa asks suddenly.

I let Mother off. All kids are standing around us; they're looking at my mother and keeping silent.

"She hasn't come yet," Mother says, "She'll come later on."

"When?" Elsa asks again.

„Soon, Elsie, soon."

"Will our mother also come?" Otto asks.

"She'll come. But not today."

"Tomorrow?"

"No, maybe a little bit later... Sonny," Mother tells Arno, "Undress me and bring snow. It seems I've got the whole of my body frostbitten."

Arno quickly takes off from Mother a shabby someone else's shawl, undoes an all-over patched padded jacket, pulls off the holey felt boots of Auntie Ida, some footwraps.

"Mu-um!" he says, „Your legs are quite white!"

"Yeah, Sunny," Mother says, "Bring snow quickly."

The Volodya's grandma Luise has come. Other grandmas have also come. They're questioning Mother. Mother is telling that the commission began to work only after three

days; there were very many people and they had to wait till they were examined. On the last day she prayed and promised God that if he'd do so that she wouldn't pass the medical examination, then she'd go home on foot that very day. And really, she didn't pass the medical examination. „My dear, where are you setting out," the doctor told her. Mother gave the aunties who were poorly dressed all her own clothing, took theirs and went off. It was getting dark already; they were trying to talk her into staying, 'cause the night was coming and sharp biting frost was outdoors, and there were also wolves to cap it all. But Mother set off – she promised God, you know, and her word had to be kept. And all the way she prayed that wolves wouldn't attack her. And now here she is, that's all well and good, but only her legs a little bit...

The Mother's legs were turning black. Below they're black, above – white. Between black and white there's a red streak. Every day the red streak is going up. All along, Mother's lying in bed. The head of the collective farm came yesterday. He saw Mother's legs and began to scold her,

"Are you a small kid, Petrovna, aren't you? Why didn't you call me at once? Long-since, you had to be taken to hospital, damn it..."

The grandpa who once rode mother on a horse sleigh to the rayon's center came to us again. He'll be bringing mother to the hospital. Her legs will be healed there and she'll come back.

Grandma Luise and grandma of Grandpa Semenych are dressing and muffling Mother warm. Then all of them together carry her over onto the sleigh. We're seeing our mother off. We aren't whining 'cause she'll be back soon.

Mother is absent for a very, very long time. I'm strolling along the street. It's lovely outdoors. There's plenty of snow and it isn't cold.

Ther're two aunties talking on the road. I'm passing by.

"... And why she didn't agree," one says.

"Who knows, maybe it's better so." the other says, "What life might be, without them, the legs."

"How do you do, aunties?" I'm greeting them.

"How do you do, sweety?" One auntie bends down to me, lifts me and kisses.

"Don't do it, put me on the ground again. I'm all grown up already."

"Oh, my deary," the auntie says, "Now you go, go." She kisses me once more in my cheek and puts me down on the ground.

"Mother is absent for long time," I want to talk to these aunties, "I'm missing her."

"Sure you're, my sweetheart, sure you're." One auntie's wiping off her tears. Maybe, she's upset that I'm missing my mother. I pity the auntie. I'm calming her,

„It's not too bad! She'll be back soon. Only her legs have to be healed." I'm saying the way Arno has told me.

"That's it, deary, that's it. You're a good boy.“

I'm keeping on going. I'm happy – I'm a good boy.

# 3. Maria

There's a big house in the rayon's center. Only children live there. There're very, very many children there. They're playing with different toys there. And there're also very, very many toys there. And they are fed thrice a day there. They're given soup, and gruel, and bread. It's good there.

Grandpa Semenych is sledging us to this house. He's sitting at the front of the sleigh. Otto's sitting beside him. He's the smallest one. Then Elsa. Then I'm sitting. And Marijke's in the back – to back me up from falling down.

There're also four opposite to us. And one boy is in the middle. Meanwhile, we're going without Arno. Arno will come later – he's promised. And he'll be living with us.

We've been sledging for quite some time already. We started as early as the day dawn was breaking; and probably it's the lunchtime by now. We've got frozen again. Grandpa Semenych brings the horse to a halt.

"Now then, let's run a bit," he says.

We're getting off the sleigh. Grandpa Semenych has also got off the sleigh and now he's going by its side. Then he's quickly going forward and from there cries,

"Ca-atch up with me! Move your legs!"

We're running along the road. If to run then you're growing warm. We're running, falling down, getting up, and running again. I fell down straight on a knoll by the roadside. I want to get up, lean with my hands against this knoll, and feel that there's something solid underneath. I rake the snow off. The face of a boy comes out.

"Maria!" I cry, "There's a boy here."

Everyone comes up to me. Maria's raking the snow off the knoll. There're two more girls lying by the boy. They've clung to each other. Maybe, it's warmer for them so. Grandpa Semenych crosses himself, and then he heaps up the snow over the children again. We seat ourselves on the sleigh and are sledging further on...

We're sledging out of the forest. A very, very big village begins. There're very, very many houses here, and there're also a lot of people here. This might be the rayon's center already now.

We're sledging up to a very, very long house. Grandpa Semenych brings the horse to a halt by the porch and helps everyone to get off the sleigh. He ushers us into the house. An auntie comes up to us there.

"Good gracious!" she tells Grandpa Semenych, "Who on earth is sending all of them to us? It's not allowed to take them, you know. Yesterday seven of such came; they were a little bit bigger. On foot, walked the whole day, all of them got frozen. And really, we aren't having any places anymore. What should I do with you?" She's gone somewhere.

It's warm in the room. We take off our warm clothing and sit down on benches. We want to sleep and to eat. Grandpa Semenych is also sitting with us. He's smoking and keeping silent.

"All right," she says, "I'll take the three of them. And the rest bring along a little bit later. I guess, after two weeks. Maybe, there'll be free places then, there a lot of the weak ones... Give the littlest ones for the time being."

She takes Otto, Elsa, and me.

"And Marijke?" I ask.

„Her afterwards," the auntie says, "next time".

I'm going to Marijke. I'll be with her. I'd better come together with her next time. The auntie takes the boy who sat in the middle of the sleigh instead of me.

Each of us is given a plate with a hot potato soup and a bit of pea porridge. It's tasty. Maybe, they always give to eat so tasty here. It would be great, if we could stay here. But after the lunch we're dressing up again and driving home.

The way back is worse. It's getting dark and cold. I'd better stayed in that house. It's warm there. And they give soup. And we'll come back home now, and there'll be nothing to eat there.

No, I hadn't to stay there. Should then Marijke be sitting alone home, when Arno will go out to work? And Arno would be feeling lonely without me as well. He himself said that he will come to us, 'cause he'd be also feeling lonely without us. How happy he'll possibly be when we come back now! We'll climb up onto the warm stove and all three of us will be sleeping there. Together!..

I might have fallen asleep. The sleigh has given a hard jerk. I've even fallen on my side. I want to lean on Marijke and to get up, but she's somehow missing.

"So where's Marijke?" I want to ask. But then a very, very loud cry bursts out back on the road. The cry breaks up, and now it's to be heard how someone's growling and yelping. As if many dogs are fighting.

The horse's snorting and running very, very fast. Grandpa Semenych is standing on his knees, steadily whipping the horse and looking back all the time. The sleigh is jerking from side to side. Grandpa Semenych brings us forward, he himself moves back. There's a rifle lying by him.

We see several gleaming lights ahead of us. This might be our village already now. The lights are getting closer. There're also lights far away back. There're plenty of them. We're sledging very fast away from them, but they're getting somehow also nearer. Now they are quite near.

But these are the dogs that are running! There're so many of them!

Grandpa Semenych fires back twice. The dogs run off the road and now they are running to us from both sides. The moon is shining, and snow is sparkling from under their paws.

Grandpa Semenych takes off his big fur cap and throws it back. The dogs are again jumping on the road. It could be heard again how they're loudly growling and fighting. While they're fighting we are now far away already.

Here is our village at last. Grandpa Semenych is sledging us speedy to his house, huddles all of us onto the porch while reloading the rifle. Already in the house we hear how he's shooting two more times. Then he comes into the house.

"What's the matter?" Grandma asks frightened.

"The wolves, damn them all." Grandpa says, "Could hardly get rid of them. Only that gal has dropped out."

All of a sudden, I'm feeling very, very warm. It's maybe so, 'cause I'm in the hut and dressed up. No, it's maybe not 'cause of that. Earlier, I also used to stay dressed up in the hut, but I've never felt like that. I'm feeling like being worn out and warm. No, it's not like that now. I'm feeling like being

warm and flimsy. 'Cause everything is sliding away from me somewhere. I'm not having anything anymore – neither arms nor legs, nothing. Maybe only my soul is left out of me. Maybe, I'm dead? But, why then my soul isn't flying up to the sky? My soul is falling down somewhere. But I'm not frightened. I'm falling down softly. As if I'm falling down on a cotton wool. And really, I'm sinking into this cotton wool, the soft, white cotton wool. But no-o, this isn't a cotton wool, this is the snow. And here is the road. On both sides of the road, the dogs are still running on snow. But no, surely these aren't the dogs. These're surely the wolves. The wolves are running on both sides of the road, and snow is sparkling from under their paws.

And there on the road, there're more wolves. They've herded together and are fighting with each other. These are they that are eating Marijke!

"Oh-oh-oh!" Marijke's crying. I'm also feeling a pain. I'm also crying. No, I'm not crying, I only want to cry, but I can't in any way. And to move from the spot where I am I can't in any way. I'm not even able to move any limb of my body. I'm only watching how wolves are eating Marijke. One wolf has grabbed her with his teeth by her face. Oh-oh-oh, terrible pain! I'm jerking to pull out my face, but I see only yellow teeth and a red tongue. I'm closing my eyes not to see anything. But the wolves are still growling, fighting and gnawing on something. They're gnawing on Marjke's bones. I can't hear how they're gnawing on bones. I'm keeping shut my ears, but all the same I hear everything. I'm feeling how sharp teeth are scratching my bones. And on both sides of the road other wolves are still running softly and quietly and snow is sparkling slowly from under their paws; and here the wolves are still growling and fighting, growling and fighting...

Where that all has vanished? It's simply dark now. And it's become very quiet. Someone's breathing beside me. Maybe, the wolves have run away and that is Marijke who's breathing near?

"Marijke!" I'm calling.

No, that's not me who's calling. I only want to call, but someone else's calling instead of me, 'cause it's not my voice.

"Fritzik, have you woken up?" I hear Arno.

"And where's Marijke?" I ask.

"Granny, Granny", Arno's calling quietly, "Fritzik has woken up."

"What? Has he come to himself?" I hear the voice of the Grandpa's Semenych grandma, "Whoopee, thank you Good gracious! I'll just light the room."

The bed is creaking. Does it mean that I'm at home? But where do we have the bed from? After all, long-long back and that was at the time when Friedrich Karlowich died, mother brought the bed back to Grandpa Semenych. It's brightening up. I'm lying on the stove. But it's not our stove; the wall is on the other side. Arno's sitting near.

"Arno, and where's Marijke?" I ask.

"Do you want to eat?" Arno says.

I'm not hungry. I'm thirsty.

"Wait, wait just a moment, you dear kiddy, I'll give you some milk," Grandmother says.

She holds out a mug to me. I want to take this mug, but I can't sit up. Nor can I hold the mug. Arno takes the mug, supports me and he's helping me to drink.

I'm still thirsty, I want to drink more.

"You shouldn't you dear kiddy." Grandmother says, "You haven't had anything in your mouth for three days run-

ning; the whole of your little tummy might have shrunk. Be patient, I'll give you some more a little bit later..."

"Now Fedjka, are you alive?" Grandpa Semenych comes out of the sitting room. He's wearing only the underpants, his beard has budged on one side.

"Alive, thank you God gracious," Grandmother says.

"What a smart boy you are!" rejoices Grandpa Semenych, "Go on, get well, I'll make skies for you. We'll go into the woods together."

Long since, I've wanted the skies, and I've also wanted to go into the woods with Grandpa Semenych. But now I don't want to go into the woods. Neither, do I want the skies. I don't want anything now.

# 4. Arno

Arno's going to go away on a trip. He wants to find our grandfather with grandmother who're Mother's grandfather and grandmother. "They've got into another village," Mother said, "because there wasn't enough place for them in our train." Also Mother said that it's far away. It's there, where the Kazakhs live.

Arno doesn't tell anyone that he wants to go away on a trip. 'Cause it's not allowed Germans to leave. If Arno would be caught, it would be very bad for him. He's said so himself.

Arno only doesn't know what to do with me. At first, he wants to ask Grandma Luise to take me to hers till I'd be housed in a children's home. But I don't want to Grandmother Luise. I want to Grandpa Semenych.

"All right," Arno says, "Only you shouldn't be whining when I'll be leaving. Agreed?"

„Agreed," I promise.

We're going then to Grandpa Semenych.

"Grandpa Semenych," I say, "house me."

"But what's the matter?" Grandpa asks Arno. Arno tells him that he wants to find our grandfather with grandmother.

"But where are you going to, Sonny, in such coldness?" Grandmother of Grandpa Semenych says, "You'd better wait till summer, at least."

Grandpa Semenych isn't saying anything. He's thinking it over for quite some time and shaking his head.

"Grandpa Semenych," I say, "take me. I'll be helping you. I'll knit socks for you. And for Grandmother, too. And I'll teach you to speak German."

Grandpa takes me on his knees. I'm petting his beard.

„All right, Fedjka," he says at last, "so be it, live here."

I'm happy. I'm hugging Grandpa Semenych very, very firmly.

Grandma has cooked potatoes in the casting pot. She puts them in a pouch. Then she wraps salt in a piece of cloth and lays it into the pouch, too. It's for Arno for the journey. Grandmother has already packed everything, but the pouch is half empty. She falls to thinking. Then she climbs up on the stove, rakes up a big scoop with sunflower seeds and emptied it out into the pouch. Now it's almost full. She ties it up, sits down on a bench and wipes off her tears with the edge of her dress.

"Good heavens, what for you are them so..." she sighs, turns to the icon and is crossing her very, very quickly.

Arno's already dressed. He ties up a cord to the ends of the pouch, swings it onto his back and passes his hands through the straps.

"Done", he says. "Thank you, Grandfather", he stretches out his hand to Grandpa Semenych. "Thank you, Grandmother", he kisses grandmother in her cheek. "I'll come soon for Fritzik."

Arno turns to me.

"Goodbye, Fritzik", he says, "Listen to Grandma and Grandpa."

I forget everything, we've agreed with Arno. I jump off the Grandpa's knees and run to Arno. I embrace his neck and start whining loudly.

"Don't go, Arno," I say, "Dear brother, don't go away. I don't have anyone anymore, you know."

Arno embraces me firmly. He's also whining.

"I'll come back very soon," he says "I'll only find out where our grandpa and grandma are, and then I'll come back for you."

"No," I say, "Father also wanted to come back, but he hasn't. And Mother hasn't come back. And you wouldn't come back."

"I'll come back, Fritzik," Arno says, "I'll only find Grandfather, our grandfather."

"I don't want our grandfather. Our grandpa will also go away and would never come back. I want to live with Grandpa Semenych."

Arno puts me down on the floor and wants to unhook my arms. But I clasp my arms round his neck even more fiercely.

"No," I'm crying, "No..."

Arno sits down with me on the bench. We're whining together. Then he takes off his hat, and undoes his coat.

„Arno, you'll stay?" I ask.

"I'll stay," Arno says and firmly clasps me to him.

With all my might I'm hugging his neck. I'm happy that Arno stays. He's good. And he's my brother. I love him. I love him more than anyone else in this world!

At night we're sleeping side by side on the stove. I'm hugging Arno, and he's hugging me. We're talking in a whisper for a long time. He's telling me fairytales.

In the morning, as I get up Arno's not by my side. Nor his coat is here.

"Arno!" I'm crying, "Arno!"

Grandma comes out from behind the stove. She's carrying something on a plate.

„Where's Arno?" I ask.

"Don't start crying, you dear kiddy," Grandma says, "Here're some potato pancakes I've baked for you, they're hot, come here, have some of them."

I jump off on the floor having only socks on and run out to the porch.

"Arno-o!" I'm crying with all my might.

It's quiet all around. Snow fell at night. New footprints are tracing from the porch of the house of Grandpa Semenych. They're leading to our tiny house. They curve there and run along the path and past the spot, where father's footprints were, to the street. They're leading to that direction where Father was taken to, where Mother was taken to, where Marijke didn't return from.

"Arno, my dear brother, and what about me?" I whisper quietly and feel that my tears are very cold.

Two big hands cover my shoulders.

"Let's go into the hut", Grandpa Semenych says, "It's cold."

# 5. Only a Black Flag above the Waters

And really, I'm feeling cold. Grandpa Semenych takes me into the hut. I'm feeling very cold. I'm trembling. Even my teeth are chattering.

"Now, drink some milk and have hot potato pancakes", Grandma's seating me at the table.

The mug is rattling in my hands. My teeth are chattering against the mug. The mug is very heavy. I can't hold it, anymore. And I'm not able to sit, anymore.

"Good Lord, again", I hear Grandma.

They're lifting and taking me somewhere. I'm taken to the snow, 'cause I'm feeling much more colder. Yes, indeed onto the snow. Onto the fresh snow that has just fallen. There, there're the Arno's footprints... Arno's footprints? Arno's gone away following these footprints? Yes, it's really so. And if I'd follow these footprints I'd catch up with Arno. Only I've got to go quicker. I've got to run. This way, quicker, quicker... The footprints could be seen very good! Now I'll be running to the end of these footprints and there'll be Arno there.

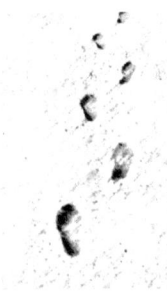

Why haven't I started running earlier? Long since, I could have caught up with Arno.

If you're running, you're warming up then. As we were on the way to the rayon's center, we also kept warming up that way. I'm not feeling cold anymore. I'm getting hot already now. I'm even sweating. But I've got to run to catch up with Arno. Only his footprints aren't to be seen anymore. It's 'cause all the snow has melted down. The snow has melted down, 'cause the sun is shining. The sun is shining very, very brightly. And the road is quite dry already. I'm still running along this road, 'cause Arno has gone away down this road. I've been running for so long already! Maybe, the whole day. No, more than that, 'cause the snow has melted down already and it's dry everywhere, you know.

Where am I now? Where I've come running to?

Oh, that's a river port! That's the river port back home on the Volga, where we all had been loaded onto a ship to bring us to a railway station and then to be shifted to a train there. We'd been loaded; and as the steamer began to cast off from the port, everyone started singing and whining. And the Russians, who were standing on the river bank looking at us, also started whining. Only the soldiers with rifles, who were guarding us, so that we embarked well, weren't whining. 'Cause they're true soldiers and the Red Army commanders never cry. They've only lowered their heads to hear the song better.

Even now I'm still hearing this song! It's singing itself from somewhere...

No-o it isn't singing itself. It's simply been staying here since our leaving. Sure it's so, it was sung to the river bank, you know; and so it's stayed by the river bank.

But why am I staying here? Why am I not running home? 'Cause our village isn't very far away from here now... And here, it's our village already. Here, it's our street. And our house. I've recognized it at once! 'Cause the whole of it is red. It's just so, as Marijke has painted it.

And there, there's the water well with a winch. And a tub is standing by the water well. Father filled it with water in the morning and Arno bathed in it in the daytime. Sure, he's also bathing in it now. And Robert, who he's going to school with, is also bathing with him. They've got only pants on and they're quite wet. Even the pouch on his back is completely wet. But they're still pouring water over each other and are guffawing, guffawing.

And there, Marijke's sitting on the porch. She's holding in her hands a big piece of red bread with butter. She's eating bread and looking at our Meta. Meta's rubbing against a corner. That means, Meta's shedding its hair and I, together with Arno, will roll up a ball...

And sugar lumps on Marijke's bread are so big! That means, she told the truth then. But I thought, she was telling stories.

But why are they sitting, as if I'm at home. I'm not at home, you know, but they aren't worrying about me. A dog might have bitten me or a bull from the collective farm might have gored me.

But maybe, they were searching after me and haven't found. Really, I was very far away, and I've been running for such a long time.

All right, I'll set foot in the courtyard by myself. No, I'd better cry and let them be searching after me.

"Ar-no!" I'm crying.

Arno stops laughing. He's looking around. But I've hidden myself away behind the gate and he doesn't see me.

„Ar-no!" I'm crying once more.

Arno starts searching after me. But would he really find me? I'm very small, you know; it's difficult to find me. I'm running into the courtyard.

"Here I am!" I'm crying loudly and running to Arno. "I've caught up with you! I've caught up with you!"

"Mama!" Arno's crying, "Fritzik has come back!"

Mother's running out of the house. Does it mean that her dear legs have been healed up already and she's gone right away home?

"My little one", Mother says and takes me in her arms, she's kissing me and whining.

"Where have you been for so long? Let's go quickly to Father, he's also waiting."

That means Father's also here. Does it mean that Mother's got to Father and they've come home together? Oh, how good it is!

We're entering the house.

"Fritz", Mother says, "have a look now, who has come to us!"

"Well, well, and who's he?" Father says, "O-oh, isn't it Fritzik? Sure, he is!" Father squats and spreads his hands widely, "Run to me!"

I'm running straight into the Father's hands. Father's picking me up and lifting me up very, very high, up to the very ceiling. I feel as if something is even being lamed between my legs. So high it is.

"Now you may throttle me a little bit", Father says.

I haven't throttled Father for so long. And now, I'm grown-up and strong. Now I'll be throttling him so that he'd yell right away.

I put my arms round Father's neck and pull it with all might to myself. Father's even closing his eyes, so strong I'm throttling him. And he says promptly:

"Ooh, Fritzik, let me off. You've become so strong! Maybe, I'll take you to school with me soon."

I'm happy. Long since, I've wanted to go once with Father to his school.

Father's going down with me on the floor. That means that we'll be wrestling with him now. I like to wrestle with my father. When at lunch I ate everything what Mother had laid on my plate I always gained the upper hand. Only today maybe Father would win 'cause I haven't eaten for a long time.

Suddenly, Arno's coming into the house. He says:

"Dad, may I take Fritzik with me to dive a bit in the cask?"

"So be it, go," Father says, "We'll be wrestling after the lunch."

I like to dive with Arno in the cask, and I'm running with him to the courtyard.

There're very, very many people who've come up from somewhere into our courtyard. I've never seen so many people, as yet. Oh, but I know all of them, it's really so!

To the right, there're only children in the courtyard. They're standing and sitting in big groups, close to each other. And my father's sitting in the middle of each group.

And grown-ups are sitting and standing to the left. Ther're also very, very many of them, and I also know each and every one of them. There's also our grandfather there. He's on horseback; in one hand he's holding a red flag and a lowered saber – in the other. And a cut off rope's hanging down from his neck. The end of the rope has dropped down and reaches the sabre.

I'm casting a glance backwards. Father has carried a chair with a high backrest out onto the porch. He's sitting very, very upright looking at me. And my mother's standing beside him; she's put her hand on his shoulder and she's looking at me. They're looking at me smiling. It means, they've asked each and every one to come over to us? How great it is!

How hot it is, really! It's so, 'cause the sun is blazing. The sun is blazing very, very strong; even my head is aching. And it's difficult to breathe. I'm breathing with the whole mouth, but all the same I can't breathe in enough, in no way. Everything has dried up in my mouth, and the tongue is such... like raw potato peels.

„Drink", I'm wheezing.


The grandma of Grandpa Semenych is handing me a scoop with water. She's putting her hand on my forehead and says,

"Good Lord, the whole of him is just glowing!"

And then again, she's fading and going away somewhere.

The sun goes on blazing in the same way. Only my legs are getting colder. Maybe, it's 'cause the water that I've drunk has gone down to the legs.

No, it's 'cause the earth in the courtyard is chilly. It's chilly 'cause it's wet. Maybe, Arno and Robert have sprinkled the courtyard with water.

No-o, it's not 'cause it's been sprinkled. It's 'cause our courtyard is sliding into the Volga. Somebody's pushing our courtyard into the Volga and it sinks in it slowly. Our courtyard is looking like a very, very big tray, you know. Only its bottom is earthen, and its edges are made of a wooden fence.

Now the whole of our courtyard is on the water. It's so wonderful! Our courtyard is just flowing on the water like a steamer!

Here on the Volga the sun is shining so brightly! It's even painful to look at it, and the whole of the sky is overcast with circlets, of different colors and the black ones. And snowflakes are falling down out of these circlets. The snowflakes are falling direct into the water. And in the water, they turn into little silvery fishes.

But alas, these aren't little silvery fishes. These are little silvery camels! At the very moment a snowflake falls down, a camelly bubbles out of the water. It would stretch out its long neck, shake off the water and would walk side by side with the courtyard. The snowflakes are falling down unceasingly, and silvery camellies with high towered heads are marching slowly on the endless waters. How beautiful!

And what's there behind the hedge? A cart is rolling there. Is this cart rolling on the water surface? Of course, it is so, right on the water. 'Cause this water is even and smooth, and the cart is rolling on it easily.

And who's been harnessed to the cart? Ouch, that's Auntie Ida! She labors hard to drag the cart's shaft pressing her shabby felt boots firmly against the water. Gaily colored tag-rags stick out from the holes of her felt boots. Auntie Ida is slowly dragging the cart, throwing backwards and aside her shabby felt boots with sticking out tagrags.

And who's there on her cart's rear? Oh, that's also Auntie Ida! It's so amazing: Auntie Ida is pulling herself.

The Auntie Ida who's sitting on the cart is looking at me. She looking at me, she's, smiling cunningly and she's luring me with her forefinger. Why she's calling me to her? Would she like to barter my felt boots? But I'm not having any felt boots; I'm barefoot, you know...

And maybe, she wants that I left our courtyard? Does she really think that I could do without our courtyard? Without our courtyard where my mother, my father, and Arno, and Marijke live – all my dearest ones who I love? How could I leave all of them? 'Cause I'm a grown-up already and must help to keep the courtyard in order... What has Auntie Ida pictured to herself?

But maybe, she'd like to call on us and she's calling me to open the gate and let her in? But it's not allowed to open the gate, you know; then water would pour into it and our courtyard would go under water and there'll be none of us left anymore. Isn't she aware of that? Then why is she calling me?

"Why are you calling me?" I ask, but she's silent.

And now I notice that our courtyard has already moved very, very far away off the Volga river bank ... No-o, maybe it's not the Volga already now. Sure, it's not the Volga! This water is different. 'Cause no bank is to be seen anywhere. There's only water all around. Where are we floating? And where are we floating to?

And how I'd run back? I do want to run back to Grandpa Semenych and his Grandma, you know. I want to run to take them, to bring them here, so that they also were here, together with us. I want they were with us 'cause I love them. And I also love Auntie Dasha – she's kind, she's taking round black shawls for everyone, let her also be with us. And the head of the collective farm, who gave us potatoes, let him also be with us. I'll bring all of them. And we all will be living together, in one courtyard. And it'll be good for all of us.

But how I'd run now back to take them? When will dock our courtyard again at the bank and take its own place?..

The cart that's being dragged by Auntie Ida is already at the gate. Auntie Ida who's sitting on the cart is again luring me with her finger. She isn't smiling anymore. She's looking at me very, very dreadfully.

„No! I won't open the gate!"

Then another Auntie Ida who's dragging the cart is knocking severely at the gate with her crooked finger. Knock. Knock. Knock.

I'm shaking my head, "No!"

She's knocking again. Knock. Knock. Knock. But now both Aunties Idas are looking at me very, very dreadfully.

"No-o!" I want to shriek out, "No-o!"

But I can't cry. Nor am I able to move. 'Cause I'm so scared that the whole of my skin has got the prickly creeps and hair on my head is moving.

"No-o!" I'm crying voiceless, but now both Aunties Idas strike together on our gate, its bolt flies off and it opens widely. I sight how the cart is rolling on and both Aunties Idas are looking at me smiling gloatingly. And water is streaming through the gate. It knocks me down whirling around the courtyard, and then turns round dragging me back to the water well. It's falling down into the well under me, having undone the chain with the bucket. But I manage in time to put my arms round the winch and I'm clinging round it with all my might.

From here, from the top I can sight everyone who was in our courtyard. The water has already reached up to their waists, but they're silent and aren't moving even. But why are they silent? They really must cry, 'cause water is really streaming into our courtyard! But why all of them are standing silently doing nothing?

"Why are you silent?" I'm crying holding firmly above the well with all my might. "Why aren't you doing anything? 'Cause our courtyard is really sinking!"

But maybe, nobody's hearing me, 'cause I'm really crying voiceless as I'm not having any voice at all, I don't know why.

I'm looking there, where children with my father were. All of them have been already flooded there. Only Father's head is to be seen above the water at some places. Father's looking somewhere far away and is also silent.

Ouch, what's this? He's really having a scar on his forehead! Exactly like the one Friedrich Karlowich had! Where has he got it from?

I'm looking the other way. But really, everyone who was in our courtyard has got such a scar! The tiny scars are even to be seen on kid's faces. I'm also having such a tiny scar; I can sight it too. That is why we aren't able to do anything and even can't cry! Only my grandpa isn't having such a scar.

And water is rising up and rising up, further on. It's covering the shoulders, splashing against the faces that aren't even shaking. Now the eyes are already looking from under the water and in the same way – they are looking at something far away. And now the scars are disappearing under the water.

There aren't scars anymore. Not a single one. 'Cause there isn't anyone left anymore.

Now, only my grandpa remains above the water. It's so, 'cause he's on horseback. He's still holding the flag in one hand and his saber – in the other.

The tiny timber beam I'm clinging to has got loose from the door-hinge and I'm floating with it in water. But I'm not being swept away; maybe, the chain has clipped the beam to the log of the wooden wellhead and it doesn't let me float away from our courtyard.

The courtyard sinks slowly deep under the water. Soon my grandpa would be under the water and I'd be left totally alone on its surface. What should I do then?.. No, I don't

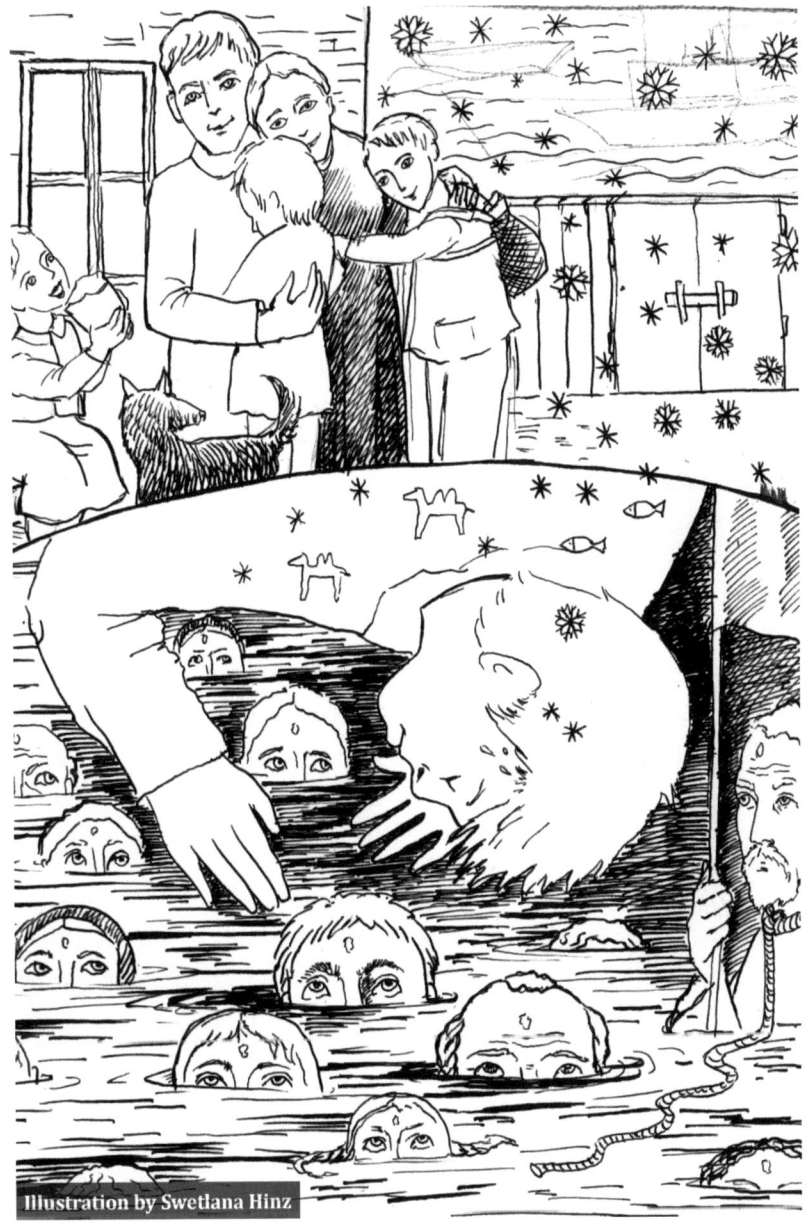

Illustration by Swetlana Hinz

want to be alone. I want to be together with all those who were in our courtyard. Indeed, I want to be together with all of them.

With all of them? Does it mean that I also will have to go under water? Yeah, sure. I must also go under the water. I simply have to let tiny beam go. 'Cause I can't swim in this water – and I'd sink under it in no time. And then I'd join all of them.

But could I dare to do it? I'm really the only one left from all of us and if I'd also go under water, then there'd be none anymore. None would even remember that we were and did have our own courtyard.

But why still to keep it in mind? And why only I should exist and remember it? I can't stand it anymore. I've just wanted already to forget it all, but I can't. Nothing can I forget. But to remember it all and to exist is also impossible for me.

What should I do then? I'm so tired of everything. I've been running for so many years to my home that is now under water! I've been on the way in other waters for so many years! And for so many years I'm trying to balance over the well with the last of my strength! I can't anymore. I also do want to go under water. To forget everything. And not to be anymore.

I'm looking at my grandpa,

"Grandpa, can I also go under water to join all of us? Why to wait? And what we are waiting for? Please, tell me that I can. Grandpa, say it! Please!"

I'm looking at my grandpa. I'm looking at my grandpa and see that the rope on his neck begins to move. Maybe, my grandpa wants to tell me something! Maybe, he wants to let me do it!

"Come on, Grandpa!"

But my grandpa is silent. It's the water that moves the rope. The water is coming up higher and higher and blankets my grandpa.

For the last time I look around. Now, there's nothing left anymore over the water, dark water. Only a black flag is there. And a rope is jerking slightly under it.

*„In the Decree of 28 August 1941… accusations of an active help and complicity in rendering assistance to German-fascist aggressors were brought against large groups of Germans — Soviet citizens.*

*The reality has revealed that these blanket accusations were baseless…"*

(From the Decree of the Presidium of the Supreme
Soviet of the USSR of 29 August 1964)

1969–1973

# Content

# Hugo Wormsbecher

*Unser Hof*

# Гуго Вормсбехер

# Наш Двор

Hugo Wormsbecher

# Our Courtyard

*Short novel*

Translation from German:
Dr. Walther Friesen

Illustrations: Swetlana Hinz
Book layout: Artem Scheller

Printing and publishing:
BoD – Books on Demand, Norderstedt